William Walker Wilkins

Does the country require a national armory and foundry west of the Allegheny Mountains;

west of the Allegheny Mountains;

If it does, where should they be located?

William Walker Wilkins

Does the country require a national armory and foundry west of the Allegheny Mountains;
If it does, where should they be located?

ISBN/EAN: 9783337727451

Printed in Europe, USA, Canada, Australia, Japan

Cover: Foto ©ninafisch / pixelio.de

More available books at **www.hansebooks.com**

DOES THE COUNTRY REQUIRE

A

NATIONAL ARMORY AND FOUNDRY

WEST OF THE ALLEGHENY MOUNTAINS?

IF IT DOES,

WHERE SHOULD THEY BE LOCATED?

PITTSBURGH:

PRINTED BY W. S. HAVEN, CORNER OF WOOD AND THIRD STREETS.

1862.

A WESTERN ARMORY AND FOUNDRY:

ARE THEY NECESSARY?

THIRTY-SEVEN years ago, under James Monroe, President, and John C. Calhoun, Secretary of War, Congress passed "an Act to establish an Armory on the Western waters." Under the Act, a commission was appointed, and three alternate sites, at and near the head of the Ohio River, selected for its location. At frequent intervals, from that time to the present, the necessity of such an establishment has been urged by the Presidents and heads of the War Department.

In 1836, Colonel Bomford, Chief of Ordnance, and Colonel Totten, recommended *two* Armories and a Foundry, to be established on the Western waters. General Lewis Cass, then Secretary of War, approved and urged the recommendation with conclusive arguments, differing only as to the number of Armories, he thinking but *one* immediately necessary. General Jackson, the President, in his Message transmitting the Reports to the Senate, said: "I think it proper to add my concurrence to the views expressed by the Secretary." In some form he called attention to the subject, in his annual Messages of 1830, 1833 and 1835. In 1835, W. Cost Johnston, from a Select Committee, made an able and exhaustive Report to the House of Representatives, in which he showed the establishment of the Armory and Foundry, to be "not only expedient, but *absolutely necessary.*" In 1836, Richard M. Johnston, chairman of the Committee on Military Affairs, made a similar Report to the Senate, with a Bill to establish a National Foundry. In these Reports are found the letters of Macomb, Barron, Shubrick, Catesby Jones, Parker, Hull, Patterson, Mahlon Dickerson, and others, each arguing the importance of the proposed establishment.

President Van Buren, in his first Message, advocated "the establishment of a manufactory of small arms west of the Allegheny Mountains upon the plan proposed by the Secretary of War (J. R. Poinsett), as tending to a much more economical distribution of the armament required in the Western portion of our country." He also recommended "the erection of a National Foundry for cannon." In his Message of 1837, he said : "The erection of a National Foundry and gunpowder manufactory, and one for making small arms (the latter to be situate at some point west of the Allegheny Mountains), all appear to be of sufficient importance to be again urged upon your attention." In short, among the records of every administration, to the present day, we can find some recommendation or recognition of the importance of having a National Armory, or Foundry, or both, erected West of the Allegheny Mountains. Most of the chief historic men of the country have, in their time, advocated their establishment. The pertinent question suggests itself—Why, then, do they not exist ? The answer is found in the insane jealousy of the respective competitors for the location, and a disposition of New England to retain a monopoly at Springfield. Members of Congress, from the pine woods of North Carolina, the mountains of Tennessee, the prairies of Illinois, the wilds of Arkansas—wherever there was an ore bank, a waterfall, a coal vein, a lead mine, or a lime kiln—each claimed for his own locality fabulous manufacturing advantages, only awaiting the "fostering care of Government" to develop them. The advocate of each failing to convince others of the superior claims of his constituency, was willing to sacrifice the public interest rather than contribute to the success of his rivals. In the present fearful emergency, when the country is torn by civil war, and threatened with destruction from abroad, it is believed that such motives will no longer be permitted to control the action of Congress.

A Cannon Foundry is distinctive from an Armory, in nearly all its requirements. The United States was among the first to decide on the importance of a *National* Foundry. It is believed that every important nation on the globe, has now one or more such establishments, *except* the United States. Our public records abound in conclusive arguments to show the necessity of a National Foundry, and but few persons, save owners of private works of the kind, have ever dissented from the proposition. Colonel Craig, late Chief of the Ordnance Department, in his Report to the Secretary of War, November 1st, 1858, said : " Every day's experience is more and more convincing of the necessity for a National Foundry of Cannon and Projectiles. The precautions which we are now compelled to adopt in order to insure, as far as possible, the use of safe and reliable materials for the fabrication of iron cannon, involve the same cost at each of the private foundries, as would be required for a National Armory of this kind. When multiplied by the number of private foundries where Government cannon are made, and where the materials and manufacture have to be severally tested, the product shows a cost, which forces of itself, exclusive of other manifest considerations, an ample argument in favor of the erection of a National Foundry. This is a matter which has been fully investigated and frequently considered by Congress, and I believe there has been little, if any, diversity of opinion in regard to its expediency."

Arguments on the subject and facts to enforce them can be extended indefinitely. We give a single illustration of the importance of a National Establishment for experiment and improvement. In 1838, Walter R. Johnston, in a letter to the Senate committee, advocating such an establishment, said: " That *cannon cannot be well cast with a core*, is a negative proposition, on which the present practice is founded of casting them *solid ;* a practice which, in the case of a 42-pounder, involves the tedious and expensive removal of more than *twelve hundred pounds* of solid cast iron, or more than *one-seventh* part of the whole weight of the casting. * * * The guns are *probably weaker*, more liable to oxidate and scale, and the boring process is expensive in respect to materials as well as to time and labor.

" That *heavy guns cannot be cast with sufficient accuracy, smoothness, and sharpness of outline, to preclude the necessity of turning, to give an exterior finish,* is another negative proposition now assumed in practice, but of which the demonstration seems to be wanting."

The first of these improvements has been made in a private foundry, and is *patented.* In regard to the second suggestion, the latest invention is to turn from the outside of the Dahlgren gun casting, nearly one-third of its weight. To perfect its ordnance as to materials, endurance, form and cost, is an important use of the National Foundry.

Is there aught in the present condition of the Nation to indicate that on this subject the opinions of our great men were erroneous? On the contrary, the enormous westward growth of population, the destruction of the Armory at Harper's Ferry, the necessities and deficiencies of the present time, unite to prove that they were right, and warn us to set about the neglected work at once. Had there been an Armory and a Foundry at the head waters of the Ohio, and an Arsenal in the Northwest, we believe our troops to-day would have been occupying every city from Cairo to New Orleans—and Tennessee, Louisiana, Arkansas, and probably Texas, would have been controlled by the Federal Government. It is said that Springfield can be extended so as to furnish all the small arms needed. Harper's Ferry, with like extension, could have done the same. But Harper's Ferry is destroyed. Who can say that Springfield is indestructible? *"Ab actu ad posse valet illatio."* What has been, may be. It does not become this great Nation to ignore the lessons of the past or the present. With a single Armory, which either accident or design might destroy—whatever may be its capacity—we are not safe. Even were it free from domestic dangers, it must not be forgotten that its proximity to the sea-coast presents inducements to a foreign foe to make whatever sacrifices might be necessary to accomplish its destruction. There should be another of equal capacity some where else. What is there to prevent? A miserable fit of false economy in Washington City? The augmented price already paid for arms, in consequence of not having the proposed works, would have erected them on the grandest scale.

What are the few hundred thousand dollars the proposed establishment will require, compared with the resources of the country, and the magnitude of the interests at stake? Erect an Armory and a Foundry on the Western waters—fill them with the necessary furnaces and machinery, and though you may never kindle a fire or turn a wheel in them, until a British fleet is seen sweeping over the Lakes to your Northern frontier, it may prove to be the salvation of the Nation. England has just taught us the lesson, that the kingdoms of Europe hold themselves always in readiness to take advantage of our weakness. The United States has demonstrated that she is stronger than any of them in *men*. Let her make herself equally strong in arms and munitions of war, and the means by which to provide them, and she may rest assured that the whole world will keep the peace with her.

Did the opinions of Jackson as to the necessity of a Western Armory and Foundry, have partly their origin in the dangerous spirit of South Carolina, and were his recommendations founded on a prophetic foresight of the present? Who can say they were not? And who can excuse the failure or neglect of the National rulers to carry out measures which they so often approved of? Let us away with the wretched spirit of jealousy and rivalry as to location, which has been the obstacle. Set about the work at once—somewhere—anywhere —only do it.

SHOULD THE WESTERN ARMORY AND FOUNDRY

DE LOCATED

AT CHICAGO?

Hon. WILLIAM WILKINS,

Chairman of Pittsburgh Committee on National Armory:

DEAR SIR—Your Committee appointed to "examine and analyze the Memorial of the citizens of Chicago, setting forth the advantages of that city as a site for a National Armory and Foundry,"

Report—That owing to the fact that the Chicago Memorial professes to draw a parallel between the advantages of that city and Pittsburgh, greatly exaggerating those of the one, and undervaluing and misrepresenting the other, we have been induced to say more in regard to Pittsburgh, than the terms of our appointment seem to require. We have, however, confined ourselves to the points made by the Memorial; and have by no means given a full statement of the advantages of the Iron City for the establishment of a National Armory and Foundry.

We entered upon the duty assigned to us, divested, as far as possible, of local prejudices, and willing to assent to the conclusions of the citizens of Chicago, if the facts and arguments presented by them justified us in so doing. In a matter so vital to the future welfare of our country, and the preservation of its liberties, as the location of the proposed Armory and Foundry, no patriot should suffer himself to be biassed by local interests. In a time of fearful exigency like the present, no true patriot can be so biassed. If, in this spirit, our plain deductions from the statements of the Memorial, our corrections

of its errors, and the comparisons necessarily instituted, have
convinced us that the public interest would be sacrificed by the
erection of an Armory and Foundry at Chicago, and confirm
us in the belief, which has existed in the public mind for forty
years—that Pittsburgh is the best place on the continent for
manufactures of iron—it is because such a conclusion is inev-
itable.

The Great Northwest—its Plea.

The Memorial sets out with a statement of the troops sent
from the Northwest, and a comparison of the population and
relative increase of the Western and Eastern States, including
Ohio with the former, and Pennsylvania with the latter. It
speaks in terms of pride of the abounding wealth of this vast
region, and of the magnificence of the commerce in which Chicago so largely shares. The writers of the Memorial can hardly
look with more satisfaction on all this than we—for on the ad-
vancement of this Great West, we and they are alike dependent. They owe their prosperity to being the Factors and
Merchants of this vast region—Pittsburgh owes hers, in a great
degree, to being its IRON MANUFACTURER. The argument of
population, then, justly used, is against the claim of the Memorial. If the people of the West (including Chicago) go
elsewhere for their bar iron, steel, and the fuel to work it with,
certainly it must be because these articles do not exist, or cannot be economically produced in Chicago ; and the larger the
population, the stronger the argument against that city as a
suitable location for works which make these articles their raw
material. That they do not manufacture iron and other metals, to any great extent in the Northwest, is admitted.

The Memorial seems to present its table of population chiefly
to support the following deductions, which we quote :

" Justice and good policy require of the Government as equal a distribution of arms, *and its expenditure for their manufacture, in the different
sections of the Union, according to population*, as can be conveniently and
safely effected." Page 4.

And on page 7 :

" It is true that manufactures of iron and other metals have not, as yet,
been established in the Northwest, on a scale so extensive as in the old

or Eastern States; but as the crude materials and the mechanical skill are found here, and *only require the fostering care of Government* to develop vast resources, we conceive this fact, so far from being an argument against our request, is, indeed, a strong reason why an Armory and Foundry should be located in this region."

The idea of equalizing the distribution of Government expenditure, according to population, cannot properly enter into the decision of this question, which is a totally different one from that of constructing roads or defenses, or distributing a treasury surplus. If it could, we might point to Pennsylvania, with New York, Ohio, Maryland and Western Virginia, clinging about her, and say: "Here are more than ten millions of your people, we demand that our share of this money shall be expended here." Your Committee reject such arguments. Every citizen is alike interested in having the arms for our common defense made and distributed in the best and cheapest manner possible. On this basis alone should the location be made, and distribution of public patronage should have nothing to do with it. Virginia, a few years back, clamored for her share of government expenditure, and an Armory was placed at Harper's Ferry. It is gone now, and with it, we believe, has departed the potency of the argument which led to so unsuitable a location.

The admission of the second paragraph quoted—that private enterprise, which collectively never errs, has not availed itself of the alleged iron advantages of that city—would prove at once that Chicago is not a suitable place for the proposed works, were it not that subsequent pages are devoted to contradicting it. The plea based on the admission, that Chicago "requires the fostering care of Government to develop vast resources," instead of being a "strong reason," seems to us so absurdly heretical as to be devoid of reason. The Government fosters the manufacturing interests of the country by judicious legislation, in the benefits of which all share. Our laws are meant to be equal, as far as human wisdom can make them so. When Congress appropriates the public money to develop the iron manufacturing resources which individual enterprise has failed to develop in Chicago, it must be at the sacrifice of the principle of equal laws on which the Government is founded.

There is nothing else in this part of the Memorial which requires notice, except the attack upon Pittsburgh ; and to avoid repetition, we will consider that elsewhere, under the heading of " Security and Geographical Position."

Iron.

The second division of the Memorial concerns *" Material required in the construction of Works and in the manufacture of Arms and Ammunition."*

The important item is IRON. The key-note is contained in the first sentence, which says : " Without fear of comparison, it may be said that no city on the continent possesses equal advantages with Chicago, as a point for the iron manufacturer, and this whether we consider the varieties of metal to be had, their unlimited supply, or the cheap rate at which they can be delivered here." To prove this assertion, then follows an enumeration and statement of the qualities of iron, which it is asserted can be taken to Chicago, so as to justify the preliminary claim : I. Lake Superior—II. Missouri—III. Pennsylvania and New York—IV. Ohio—V. Tennessee—VI. Indiana—VII. Wisconsin—VIII. Scotch Pig.

I. *Lake Superior Iron.*

Of these, Lake Superior seems to be the chief reliance. Passing by the fact, which is proved by your Committee on Iron, that the Lake Superior metal will not make cannon, we remark, 1st. That notwithstanding the asserted proximity of Chicago, nearly all the iron made on Lake Superior is consumed in Pittsburgh, Detroit and Cleveland. 2d. That more than three times as much of the ore of Lake Superior is smelted in Pittsburgh and its vicinity, as is smelted at the mines or on the shores of Lake Superior; and not a pound of the ore is smelted in the city of Chicago or the State of Illinois. Our Pittsburgh manufacturers bring the ores of Lake Superior, of Missouri, of Canada, and Lake Champlain, to this city, and by means of our cheap labor and excellent fuel, convert them into metal here at a less cost than it can be made for at the mines. In 1859, forty vessels were employed in bringing us the Lake Superior ore; in 1860, over seventy, and in 1861, the number is largely increased. None of them bear their treasure to Chicago, with its "superior advantages for manufacturing iron to any city on the continent." Why is it? Simply because the advantages exist only in the imagination of the authors of the assertion quoted. Lake Superior iron, or Lake Superior ore, will never go to Chicago to be manufactured, because the proper fuel does not exist there. If the fuel could be economically transported to the iron, then the coal would be carried to Marquette, instead of the ore being brought to Ohio and to Pittsburgh. What is true of the ore and coal, must be true, in a still more striking degree, of the pig metal to be reduced to other forms, for the disproportion in bulk between them is greater. But even if it were possible to transport economically the coal and the iron to some half-way station, a glance at the map will show that Chicago is not the place. The vessels would meet midway on their journey to Chicago, and traverse side by side the Straits of Mackinac and the whole length of Lake Michigan. To what end? To foster the imaginary resources of Chicago at the expense of the Government.

II. *Missouri Iron.*

This iron is also justly praised, but the Memorial, with its usual accuracy, says:

"Their 'best charcoal No. 2 iron,' is the kind almost exclusively used by the Pittsburgh manufacturers, even at the long distance of transportation, for making their No. 1 boiler plate, and other tough irons. This iron can now be had at the mines at the low price of $16 per ton, and the freight will not exceed $5 per ton, making this valuable iron cost, delivered in Chicago, from $20 to $22 per ton."

We produce here over 10,000 tons annually of boiler and sheet iron alone, to say nothing of other tough irons, while the entire production of the Iron Mountain and Pilot Knob furnaces is less than 10,000 tons, of which the "No. 2 charcoal" is but a small portion; hence, there cannot be very much taken to Chicago. The cost of delivering it there, if Government should create a demand, is necessarily given as a surmise at $5. We state, as the experience of years, that it costs from $3 to $5, according to the season, to deliver it here, and that this city is its great market. The ore is also brought here in quantities, and made into iron cheaper than it can be made at home.

III. & IV. *Soft New York and Pennsylvania and Ohio Irons.*

The localities indicated by the names, show that these can be brought to Pittsburgh more cheaply than taken to Chicago, and the fact exists, that nearly every brand of their iron is constantly on sale in this market.

V. *Tennessee.*

The statement is that this metal can be bought in Chicago at $20 per ton. The cost of freighting it to St. Louis, we remark, is about the same as to Pittsburgh. The freight between St. Louis and Chicago, a few sentences back the Memorial estimates at $5 per ton; hence, the iron must cost $5 more per ton in Chicago than in Pittsburgh. Your Committee account for the low price named, by supposing that some unfortunate furnaceman, attracted by the proclaimed advantages, sent a few tons of his metal to Chicago, and finding no demand, offers to sell at a sacrifice. Be this as it may, we have before us sales of Tennessee iron in this city, during the last two months, amounting to over 700 tons, at $19 per ton. We have far larger sales of better brands considerably below that figure.

VI. & VII. *Indiana and Wisconsin.*

These comprise the product of two or three furnaces. The former, the Memorial says, is used for "light castings;" of the latter, "it is a soft brittle iron." The description indicates their value to a National Foundry and Armory.

VIII. *Scotch Pig,*

Which possesses precisely the qualities of some of our home irons, is not valuable to the manufacturer of bar iron, and is in no case used for making cannon. It can be bought here as cheaply as in Chicago.

The concluding paragraph tells us: "The cost and supply of steel and wrought iron are proportional to those of cast iron," and naively adds, "it will not be necessary to go into details on this subject." The details would show that the supply of these articles is nearly all purchased in the city of Pittsburgh. To illustrate further the absurdity of the Chicago pretensions, we quote from the letter of a member of the Committee to Hon. J. K. Moorhead, which disposes also of the *lumber, copper, skilled labor, health, food* and *population* claim of the Memorial:

"There is a greater variety of Pig Metal sold in Pittsburgh than in any other market in the United States. The number of the *best* brands found here is greater than in any other market, and their average price is lower than any where else. To illustrate: Scotch Pig may possibly be cheaper in New York City; Tennessee may be cheaper on the Cumberland River, and Lake Superior at Marquette; but the three brands are always found side by side in Pittsburgh, at a lower price than they ever can be at the point of production of either. The mixture of the three makes a better iron than either alone. The strongest metal is made from mixtures. Each manufacturer of bar iron, castings, or steel, by mixing the product of different furnaces, in proportions the result of his own experience, is able to produce an iron exactly suited to its intended use.

"Mr. Isaiah Dickey, iron commission merchant, informs me that while receiving consignments from Tennessee and from Georgia, he shipped the Georgia metal, before removing it from the landing, back to a foundryman in Nashville, Tennessee. The explanation is, that the foundryman needed metal possessing certain qualities with which to modify peculiarities of the Tennessee iron, and sent his order to Pittsburgh. The merchant knowing the Georgia metal to possess the required qualities, immediately started it back over the route it had just traveled. This fact illustrates, at the same time, the importance to the manufacturer of access to the different brands, and the fact that Pittsburgh is the place to which he naturally sends his order, knowing that here every variety is found. That it is essential to the success and proper economy of a Foundry and Armory, that it should be located in the midst of the greatest variety of irons, is well understood by ordnance officers, and is proved by their recorded experience."

Bar Iron and Steel.

"The production of Bar Iron in Pittsburgh is far more than double that of any other city in the Union; and there is more Steel made here—exclusive of the puddled or semi-steel—than in all the other cities of the United States together. We produce steel of qualities adapted to every purpose, from the finest cutlery and small arms, to rifled field artillery. Several of our establishments have been entirely successful in making cast-steel cannon. The opinion is growing among ordnance officers, both in Europe and America, that the time is not distant, when most of the field artillery and much of the light naval armament of the world, will be of steel. The great Prussian manufacturer, Krupp, has demonstrated that it is altogether the most durable and the safest material—advantages which more than compensate for the increase of cost. Its great strength will allow cannon to be made as light as is desirable. Puddled Steel, which is also coming into use for ordnance, is extensively produced—and Pittsburgh has a greater number of furnaces, such as are used in its manufacture, than any other city. For the cheap production of Ingot or Rolled Copper, and the excellence of the quality produced, Pittsburgh is not excelled elsewhere."

Timber.

"A circle drawn with a radius of say seventy-five miles, Pittsburgh being the centre, contains more valuable Timber, and of greater variety, than is found in an equal area around any city west of Pennsylvania. The region included—embracing as it does the alluvial bottom of three rivers, part of the Allegheny Mountain slopes and summits, and extending into the region of the Northern pine—furnishes the Oak, Walnut, Maple, Hickory, Ash, Beech, Elm, Chestnut, Pine, &c., in the greatest perfection."

Leather.

"The same area produces more tanned Leather (an indispensable war material) than any similar area in the West. The hides of which it is manufactured are mostly brought from west of the Mississippi, to reach our cheap labor and abundant supplies of bark. There is no equal area of country, with better or cheaper transportation facilities, from its centre to all its parts."

Expense of Living.

"The *expense of living* is as low in Pittsburgh as in any other city west of the mountains, and lower than any west of Columbus. This is sufficiently proved by the cheapness of labor, the general comfort in which our mechanics live, and the comparative low price at which the product of our workshops is sold."

Skilled Labor—Population.

"In the supply of *skilled labor in iron*, Pittsburgh offers advantages which cannot be equaled elsewhere. In showing this fact, it is necessary to correct an important error as to the population of our city, which exists in some quarters. The Chicago Committee state it at 49,220. The corporate limits of Pittsburgh comprise the triangular space between the Allegheny and Monongahela rivers. This space was fully populated years ago, and is the Pittsburgh of the official census reports. Adjoining and surrounding it on all sides are the various boroughs and the city of Allegheny, the whole making up what is commonly known as Pittsburgh. Allegheny alone contains 31,536 inhabitants; Manchester, Birmingham, Lawrenceville, and the other manufacturing suburbs, have 31,845—making the total population of Pittsburgh 112,591. With this correction, it is a pleasure to accept in population, as in all other things, the comparison which our Chicago friends have so happily instituted:

Population of Chicago, - - - - 109,263
        " of Pittsburgh, - - - 112,591

"This increase," says the Chicago Committee (page 16), "so largely in favor of Chicago over other cities, it is claimed is on account of her central position, ease of access, and many avenues to concentrate to and distribute from to a very large territory, embracing several States"—or, in other words, her *commercial facilities.* The increase of population in Pittsburgh is due solely to her *manufacturing advantages,* incidentally including cheap and rapid transportation to all parts of the country.

In Chicago (page 16 of Memorial) there are 2,866 hands employed in iron works, steam engines, &c. In Pittsburgh there are over 12,000 hands working in iron alone. Yet our Chicago friends (on page 21 of their Memorial), after claiming superiority over the Iron City in all other particulars, say, "In supply of skilled labor we are fully equal to Pittsburgh." Your Committee, indorsing the facts and figures of the above extract from the letter to Gen. Moorhead, leave them to suggest their own inferences, and proceed to the consideration of the next important item.

Health.

Pittsburgh is free from epidemics and malaria. Her health statistics show a result so superior to that of any other city, as to astonish those who have not by actual residence acquired a personal knowledge of the fact. This superiority, attributable probably to the peculiarity of her atmosphere, added to advantages of location and climate, is perhaps the reason why the Memorial omits Pittsburgh in the table of health statistics. From the careful statement of Dr. J. L. Duncan, Physician to the Board of Health, the deaths in the city of Pittsburgh, including still-born and accidents, were—

In 1856,... ....1.48 per cent.
" 1857,................... ....1.59 "
" 1858,................... ....1.45 "
" 1859,...1.39 "
" 1860,...1.42 "

The average for the five years is 1.46 per cent. According to the Memorial, the Chicago average for the same time is 2 per cent.

The mortality table of the Memorial, makes Chicago superior to all other cities in this particular, and equal to Philadelphia. In view of the prevalence of malarious diseases in Chicago, we apprehend there is a mistake somewhere.

Fuel and Motive Power.

Under the heading "Supply and Cheapness of Motive Power," the Memorial begins thus: "The coal required for the Armory and Foundry would be (unless the Government

2

means to smelt its own iron,) *for the purpose of motive power;*" and then comes a glowing description of the coal fields of Illinois, the richness of which, they say, has been proved beyond question, by several learned professors. That the Government *may* in the future wish to smelt its own iron, is an important consideration in locating the works. If, as is here implied, our Chicago friends have discovered a mode of melting iron for cannon, or forging gun barrels, and the various parts of small arms, without fuel, we yield the matter at once, for in this city we cannot even make a horse shoe without heating the iron. If, on the other hand, they do use coal for these purposes, why not use their own, which is so *rich* and so *cheap?*

Where Chicago gets Coal.

From the Report of the Board of Trade, we learn that there was received in Chicago, during the year 1860, 131,080 tons of coal, *from all sources.* Of this, the small quantity of 13,424 tons was received by rail road and canal from the Illinois coal field. The rest, being 117,656 tons, was received by the lake, and *came from the coal fields of Pennsylvania and the adjoining county of Mahoning, in Ohio.*

From page 4 of the Chicago Memorial, we copy the following statement:

"The coal is of the bituminous variety, and contains from forty-eight to sixty-two per cent. of fixed carbon.

The price at Chicago is:

Pure lump, per ton,	$2 00
Nut size of same,	1 50
Fine,	1 25

The best qualities of Ohio coal are sold at Chicago for $3.25 to $3.50 per ton in large lump, and in form suitable for blacksmithing and smelting, at from $2.25 to $2.50 per ton.

The best Lehigh large lump, $5; Pittston, Scranton,   ; River Lehigh, $4; fine, of best quality for blacksmithing, $2."

And in contrast with this, we copy from page 54 of the "Annual Report of the Chicago Board of Trade, January, 1861," the following table, remarking, that to the price by cargo, must necessarily be added the cost of delivery. "Hard," means anthracite.

Table showing the Prices of Coal by the Cargo, and Yard Prices, monthly, in 1860.

MONTH.	Date.	Price by Cargo. Bituminous.	Yard Prices. Bituminous, at Retail.	Yard Prices. Hard.
January....................	1	....	$5 75@6 00	$7 75@8 00
February	1	....	5 75 6 00	7 75 8 00
March..	1	....	5 75 6 00	7 75 8 00
April	1	$3 63@3 85	5 75 6 00	7 75 8 00
May..	1	3 55 3 60	5 25 5 50	6 25 6 50
June.....................	1	3 45 3 50	5 25 5 50	6 25 6 50
July..	1	3 45 3 50	5 00 5 25	5 75 6 00
August................	1	3 45 3 50	4 50 5 00	5 75 6 00
September	1	3 75 3 80	4 50 5 00	5 75 6 00
October................	1	4 15 4 20	5 00 5 50	6 00 7 00
November...............	1	4 50 4 75	5 50 6 00	8 00 10 00
December.	1	....	6 00 6 50	10 00 10 50

Your Committee accept the table as strictly correct, and deem it unnecessary to enlarge upon the inference which inevitably follows a comparison with the figures of the Memorial. The price of coal in Pittsburgh is:

Large Lump,...$1 12 per ton.
Nut Coal,............................... .... 66 "
Fine,.............. .... 40 "
Cannel Coal,........ .... 2 00 "
Coke,.. 4 per bus.

Nor are these prices for an inferior article, but for the best fuel in the known world.

We conclude our comments on coal with a further quotation from the letter to Gen. Moorhead:

"Pittsburgh coal is found in every port—from Buffalo to Superior City—from New Orleans to St. Paul—either for consumption or in progress of transportation from the rivers to the interior."

Where St. Louis, Peoria and Rock Island get their Coal.

"*Pennsylvania*—and the adjoining county of Mahoning, in Ohio—*supplies the coal which is used to smelt iron ore, or melt pig metal, in all the cities and towns west of this State.* Mr. J. B. Morgan, Jr., one of the numerous dealers in coke, writes to me: 'I ship coke by rail road to the following, among other points: NEW BRIGHTON, Salem, Massillon, Canton, Mansfield, Galion, Lima, Newark, COLUMBUS, Piqua, Urbana, CLEVELAND, Monroeville, DAYTON, Springfield, Kenton, Frederickstown, Sidney, Mount Vernon, Martinsville, RICHMOND, IND., Fort Wayne, INDIANAPOLIS, CHICAGO, ILL.' Mr. Wm. II. Thompson, of the Vulcan Foundry and Machine Shop in ROCK ISLAND, ILLINOIS, in a letter about supplies of coke, of the 18th November, says: 'I have had coke from Pittsburgh, both by river and rail (1,500 miles by river and 700 by rail). * * * I had to pay one hundred and sixteen dollars for freight alone, on five hundred bushels, which makes very expensive coke.' A highly respected firm in PEORIA, ILL., writes October 2d, in reply to mine: 'We called on one of our principal foundrymen; he says they use the anthracite or Lehigh coal for melting, and the Blossburg, Pa., coal for blacksmithing. The Illinois coal is too full of sulphur for any use, except for country blacksmithing. * * * He thinks the quality of our coal is about the same as the Rock Island.' The foundries and machine shops in the West, which do not use Pittsburgh coal or coke, substitute anthracite coal from Eastern Pennsylvania. Even the Memorial of the citizens of Chicago, setting forth the advantages of that city as a site for a National Armory and Foundry, recognizes the fact (on page 18), where it gives the prices of Ohio, Lehigh, Pittston, Scranton, &c., and designates them as *suitable for 'blacksmithing and smelting,'* at from two to five dollars per ton. The Illinois coal, 'the richness of which, for steam and motive power, is established beyond question,' is quoted at $1.25 to $2.00, per ton. That which is, to quote their own words, 'suitable for blacksmithing and smelting, comes from Pennsylvania.' The Government cannot establish a Foundry and Armory west of the Pittsburgh coal field, without being dependent on that field or the more distant anthracite region for its fuel. It *must* come to Pittsburgh for all the coal to melt its metal or work its forge fires. Even the most inferior quality of coal for raising steam, costs, in Chicago, thrice as much as engine coal does delivered at the furnace doors in Pittsburgh."

Fire Brick and Building Materials.

For lining blast furnaces, melting furnaces, &c., the only really good Fire Bricks west of the mountains are produced around Pittsburgh. Chicago is supplied from this city and from New York. The furnaces at the Iron Mountains in Missouri, when the writer was last there, were lined with Pittsburgh bricks; and the fire bricks used on Lake Superior are transported either from Pittsburgh or the State of New York. The item is omitted in the Chicago Memorial; and to show its importance to an iron manufacturing city, we state that in 1857 (the last year of which we have the accurate figures,) the annual consumption in the Pittsburgh rolling mills alone was 2,095,000 fire bricks, and 5,040 tons of fire clay. The bricks cost from $9.00 to $30.00 per thousand.

In Stone, Brick, Lime, Sand, Lumber and Iron for building, Pittsburgh abounds—and all her materials are excellent and cheap.

Chicago's Geography.

We come now to consider the Memorial headings, " *Geographical position of Chicago and means of communication with other points,*" and " *Security from attack by Foreign or Domestic Enemies*"—and under this heading, a paragraph on the 6th page, before alluded to. It states that the Northwest has been neglected, and cannot be compensated for the neglect

" By establishing another National Armory in any of the Eastern States, even if located at Pittsburgh, on the western slope of the Alleghenies. If the situation of Pittsburgh were further removed than it is from the boundaries of the States in rebellion, and from Harper's Ferry, where an Armory was captured, without an effort from loyal States made for its defense—if the navigation of the Ohio River were less uncertain, and the single trunk of rail road connecting that city with the West less exposed than it is, it would be still true, that, so far as the Northwestern States are concerned, they can be more surely, cheaply and rapidly supplied with arms from New York or New England, than from that point."

We have suggested elsewhere that the proposed Armory and Foundry is not projected for the purpose of distributing public funds "according to population," nor to "develop manufacturing resources" of a particular city—so neither is it to compensate any section for real or supposed neglect. To common sense, any argument on this proposition is unnecessary.

How much truth there is in the rest of the quotation we will show. We have before us a statement exhibiting the stage of water in the Ohio River for eleven years, which gives an average of 109 days in each year as too low for ordinary freighting—47 days of which admitted of navigation by small steamers. According to a statement made in 1857, by Hon. J. K. Moorhead, President of the Slackwater Navigation on the Monongahela, during ten years that river was obstructed by ice an average of 15½ days per annum; and "the Ohio was obstructed by ice nearly the same length of time." The Lake navigation to Chicago is usually closed for the winter about the 10th of November, and resumed about the middle of April—an interruption of over five months. The Ohio River is then useless for navigation 77 days, and the Lake route to Chicago over 150 days per annum. The Ohio River is susceptible of being made continuously navigable through the year, and probably will be so improved—the Lake can never be changed.

As to the "*single trunk*" of railway from Pittsburgh to Chicago: the map *which accompanies the Chicago Memorial* shows four trunk lines by which we can reach Chicago. When our partially completed roads are finished, five roads leading toward that city will leave Pittsburgh, and each connect with the rail road net-work of the West. A glance at the *same* map shows *a single railway line* from Buffalo to Cleveland, close along the Lake shore, and exposed at a hundred points to attack from a Northern foe. When the Lake navigation is open, Pittsburgh is 140 miles distant from it at Cleveland by rail; New York City is 459 miles from it at Dunkirk, which is still 143 miles further from Chicago than is Cleveland; West Point, New York, is 326 miles from it; and Springfield, Mass., is 400 miles from it at Buffalo, which is still 183 miles east of Cleveland.

The rail time between Pittsburgh and Chicago is 18½ hours—between New York and Chicago it is 36 hours. With all these figures, accessible to every one who can read a Traveler's Guide, the Memorial asserts that "the Northwestern States can be more *surely, cheaply* and *rapidly* supplied with arms from New York or New England, than from Pittsburgh!"

On page 9 we have the following table :

To Cairo from Chicago,	365 miles;	from Pittsburgh,	686 miles.
" St. Louis "	281 " " "		630 "
" Quincy "	268 " " "		648 "
" Rock Island "	183 " " "		650 "
" Dunkirk "	188 " " "		655 "
" Pr. Du Chien "	249 " " "		707 "
" La Crosse "	280 " " "		747 "

We have shown elsewhere that the material used in an Armory at Chicago would go from Pittsburgh or the East; and we accept the above table (without examination into its accuracy) to show, that from all points in the West south of Chicago, the distance which the iron and steel must travel, either in the bar or finished implement, would be increased by manufacturing it there. For example : Pittsburgh to Chicago, 467 miles; thence to Cairo, 365 miles—total, 865 miles—from which deduct 686, and the extra distance is 146 miles. For a statement of the transportation facilities of Pittsburgh to all parts of the country, we refer to the Pittsburgh Memorial to Congress.

Security.

The remaining topic of the Memorial is " *Security.*" Absolute security from foreign attack should, we think, be a *sine qua non* with the Government in selecting the location. Our own Government has just illustrated against Port Royal what can be done by even a wooden fleet. With this experience before us, and in view of the late experiments in iron-clad vessels, we cannot think the Government will ever establish an Armory and Foundry on the Lake Shores. Certainly it ought not to be thought of while England holds the Canadas. The Memorial tells us, "Lake Michigan can readily be rendered inaccessible to hostile fleets, by fortifications at the Straits of Mackinac;" but that is not conclusive. General Lewis Cass (than whom there can be no better authority in aught that concerns the Northwest), in his able report on coast defenses, made while Secretary of War, said : "As to the Straits of Michilimackinac, they are too broad to be defended by stationary fortifications." (24th Cong., 1st Sess., Doc. 243.) If it is said the improvements in ordnance and the range of projectiles modify General Cass' conclusion, it may be replied, that the improvements which render vessels invulnerable more than compensate, and his opinion is still correct.

Chicago is, perhaps, the least defensible of all the Lake cities. The country, on the edge of which it is situated, says the Memorial (page 5), "is a vast plain, without natural barriers to defend it, or any of those mountain fastnesses, which in other countries have often proved the strongholds of liberty and national independence."

Pittsburgh, as any one is aware, who has ever entered its vicinity, is precisely one of those strongholds. Situated nearly 400 miles from the sea-board, and over 100 miles from the lake shore; separated from the former by mountain chains, and from the latter by a rugged country, with hundreds of intersecting streams, either of which could be made the grave of an invader, should his armies escape the perils of landing on our shores—it is inaccessible to a foreign foe. Besides this, its peculiar situation among the hills, easily approachable only by the valleys of its three rivers, adapts it for defense in a remarkable degree. Three of these overlooking hills command every possible approach, and a few weeks labor in fortifying them, would render the place absolutely impregnable. The commission of army officers employed to examine it in June last, pronounced it naturally the strongest position they knew of in the country. Their Report is on file at the War Department.

Inferences.

After what has been said, you will listen with astonishment to the following extract from the last page of the Memorial:

"By those who may take the pains to compare the figures we have given, with the statements of the Memorial of the citizens of Pittsburgh, it will be perceived that, in regard to building materials, lumber, iron, copper, lead, coal for smelting, provisions, transportation and security, the advantages are in favor of Chicago. In supply of skilled labor, they are fully equal; while, as respects motive power alone, Pittsburgh has the advantage in the cost of bituminous coal. It requires but a little calculation to show that this difference in the cost of coal, for one purpose, is more than counterbalanced by the other considerations which we have named."

We are at a loss which most to wonder at, the recklessness of the assertion, and the boldness of the inferences of the Memorial, or the child-like faith of its authors in the want of intelligence of those to whom it is addressed.

Chicago claims to be the largest grain and lumber market in the West, and all will admit the claim. Unfortunately for their ambition, Rodman and Dahlgren guns are not made of corn, nor are rifles and sabres made of pine boards. When they come to be made of these materials, Chicago may properly be selected as the site for a National Armory and Foundry.

Leading branches of manufactures, as well as of commerce, aggregate in the locality best suited to them. The Government has, in this fact, an unerring guide to the proper location for its works. That point which has attracted to itself the greatest number of like establishments, must be the best for any manufactures of iron. The collective judgment of men, guided by self-interest, never errs, and their cumulative testimony of fifty years, proclaims PITTSBURGH pre-eminently the IRON CITY.

Your Committee remark, that in this Memorial there is a confusion as to the purposes of a Foundry, an Armory, a Fort, and an Arsenal. Our Western friends certainly know that an armory is not a fort, and that an arsenal is not necessarily a foundry. We agree with the Memorial, that Chicago should be defended by a fort, or works of some kind, and that the Northwest should have an Arsenal for the deposit and distribution of arms. The Arsenal should be on Rock Island, which is a better point than Chicago for distribution, South and North—is far enough from the Lake shore to need no forts to defend it, and is in every way calculated for that purpose. We hope that the same legislation which establishes an Armory and Foundry at the most suitable place, will locate an Arsenal on Rock Island.

All of which is respectfully submitted.

FELIX R. BRUNOT,
JAMES M. COOPER,
GEO. H. THURSTON,

December 26th, 1861. *Committee.*

The following Letter relative to the location of a National Armory and Foundry, from the Hon. Judge Wilkins to the Hon. J. K. Moorhead, although not intended for the public eye, is, by permission of its venerable author, here presented in connection with the foregoing views, as eminently confirmatory thereof:

Letter of Hon. William Wilkins.

HOMEWOOD, December, 1861.

MY DEAR SIR—Does not your experience in life (not quite so long as mine,) teach you, that any man of a little skill can very readily find an excuse for his delinquency? I may claim some little skill, but I am driven at this moment to a very ordinary apology—the spirit of procrastination—for my delay in giving a reply to a note received from you a long time since. I might further say, in extenuation of my omission, that I have been indulging in the dream of my ability to make a visit—my last visit—to that city (now almost in the state of actual siege), formerly the place of my political residence. My eighty-second year has commenced its course. Whence, then, is to come the capacity, the physical power, to encounter the journey? Whilst the question may tinge the mind with some little melancholy reflection, yet, it should fill mine to overflowing gratitude to Providence for the preservation in which His beneficent hand has, for so many years, continued to hold me.

The proposed establishment of a National Armory west of the Allegheny Mountains, or, rather, "the inquiry into the expediency of such an establishment," very naturally, and with great propriety, wakens up and demands the attention of the population of the city of Pittsburgh.

The language of the Congressional resolution; the condition of our distracted country; the universal cry of its people for weapons of warfare; the barren position of the North as to the essential munitions either of defense or annoyance, produced by the hidden and secretly devised treason, even of cabinet ministers—forcing us to resort for supplies to European countries, and more particularly to that country now in an angry temper, talking of menace intended to die away without effect; the destruction of the Southern Armory by the very traitorous community to whom its locality was given as a State favor and benefit—all these facts and considerations combine to satisfy us, that, at all events, a second National Armory is decided upon; and that its location, which we may equally consider as certain, will be at a proper distance from the similar works at Springfield, somewhere west of the Allegheny Mountains, in the midst of the natural wealth, resources and rivers of the Great West.

Let your honorable Committee too, take heed, that the exposure to war is stamped upon the destiny of every earthly nation. No government, however weak, or however powerful, can, at all times, escape from the scourge and calamity of dreadful hostile military contests, carried on either in defense, for conquest or for revenge. The Government of the United States—its construction—its principles of equal and impartial freedom—its just administration—our social, personal and commercial intercourse—the vast wealth and prosperity flowing from our confederacy—all combined, have not been adequate to save us from treason, and from the disaster even of civil war.

The resolution under the authority of which you are acting, plainly indicates the absolute public necessity of a second great National Workshop. It also, impliedly, forbids all contemplation of a revival of the old factory, or the establishment of a new one upon the ludicrously so-called "sacred soil" south of the Potomac River; but it hardly imposes any limits of inquiry, when it permits you to range over the entire prolific and interesting region of the Valley of the Ohio.

Further, am I wrong in coming to the conclusion, that the resolve of the House of Representatives authorizes the Committee, if it should decide upon an affirmative report, to go further, and select and decide upon the place or site, designated by economy and essential facilities, for the establishment of the great workshop called for by the exigency of the country? Without going that far, your work is but half executed. It follows, impliedly, indeed plainly, that in your report you should answer the very natural question, *Where* do you locate the establishment?

The entire wide West, excited, starts up and arrays its files and its columns, not in arms, but in honorable and friendly contest, under the bloodless armor of honest argument, of facts and facilities, of transportation and intercourse, of a community engaged and skillful in mechanics and manufactures, of fuel, particularly of the vast advantages in metal, and of that crowning circumstance, the ample possession of that overruling power which gives name to the age in which we live, and covers the waters of the world with its availability! In such a *western* contest, can the city of Pittsburgh, in justice to herself and the country, remain passive and a mere looker-on? No. She has become a competitor, and so continues, in full confidence that she possesses the site that combines more and greater advantages to the Government for the proposed national establishment, than any other locality in the region named in your resolution.

Let a friend, an adversary, or a stranger, in reference to this inquiry, turn to the map of the country, and he will at once, and very naturally, put his finger upon the "*Fork*," so called and so marked by General Washington, at the head of the Ohio.

A Memorial, accompanied by a map prepared and printed by a Committee appointed by the citizens of Pittsburgh, has been distributed at Washington amongst the members of Congress. I signed that instrument, satisfied of its truthfulness and integrity. You are aware I have no claim to the credit of being an artist, a mechanic, or a manufacturer, but you cannot be a stranger to the close and long attention I have paid to the facilities and resources of Pittsburgh, and the working character of its people. You must also well understand, that, in my present age—in my idle retirement—lost to the impulse of ambition—engaged in the working or production of no raw material, and concerned in no manufacture, I can have no personal interest or speculation in view. I may, therefore, under this state of disinterestedness, go on further and say to you, that since that Memorial was written, additional facts of value might be added to what we have already said.

The Pittsburgh and Connellsville Rail Road Company have proceeded with their work, and now have brought their road

into the city of Pittsburgh, thus opening to us, uninterrupted-
ly, in addition to our slackwater navigation, the rich valley
lying above us, and all the resources and many facilities of the
Monongahela and Youghiogheny rivers. This road is referred
to in our Memorial, but I cannot avoid mentioning the positive and distinct fact of the completion of the Pittsburgh ter-
minus of it, and that its depot is in the heart of the city.
You, sir, can well, and with full personal knowledge and experience, affirm to your honorable colleagues, the marked use-
ful bearing of this circumstance upon the supply and the
cheaper cost of the essential material of fuel. I do not hesi-
tate, also, to ask you to give your unqualified assurance of the
extraordinary richness, purity and abundance of that mineral
in the hills of the two rivers, at the bases of which the rail
road runs parallel and contiguous to the slackwater navigation.

I may also here, in repetition, name that marked and important article, the manufacture of Steel—upon which a separate
paper will be laid before you—not confining it to the superior
article in the making of edge tools, but comprehending cast
steel ordnance, at this moment in construction in the city of
Pittsburgh. In turning to page 15 of the Chicago Memorial,
comprehensive in its range (I must presume for political purposes), over the Lakes and so many of our States, we find the
word "steel" only once used, and then in reference to the
"*cost of its supply*" from distant parts. I think it a little
odd that this item, so indispensable, whether used alone, or as
an ingredient which enters, with others, into the compound
and union of different substances necessary to the production
of metallic weapons of war, has not been prominently placed
before you by our Illinois neighbors, in the account about to
be settled between us. It is strange that this essential ingredient in the construction of muskets, rifles, carbines, revolvers,
pistols, swords, and bowie knives, if you please, should be dis-
regarded and slurred over, whilst they enter into a detailed
display of their stone, beautiful cream-colored brick, wood and
lumber, shingles and lath, manufactured articles of wood,
agricultural implements, carriages and wagons, furniture, sash-
doors, barrels and wooden ware !

I might here refrain, as an analysis of that adroitly and exceedingly well written paper will be handed to you. Still, let me make a remark or two. The military commission of 1825 considers the water power at Beaver of importance, because *situated upon the Ohio river.* The Chicago Committee refers to this stream, and seems to regret the want of uniformity in its navigation. Like the Chicago, the Illinois, and their canals, it is liable to frost, depression and fullness. It has the ordinary characteristics of all our rivers. Our opposing Memorialists should have quoted the sarcasm of John Randolph —"that it was an abortion of nature ; for, one-half the year it was dry, and the other half frozen up." Still, it does not require a Roanoke wit to give us a proper comprehension of the universal utility of the navigation of the Ohio river—its great value to the entire Nation—its peculiar necessity, adaptation and resources to the establishment of a National Armory and Foundry in the Western Valley, west of the Allegheny mountains—not " on the slope of the Alleghenies."

Let Pittsburgh, especially, whilst she mourns over the loss of the navigation of the beautiful Ohio in the more favored waters of the Chicago and the Illinois, not forget the millions and millions of tons of "*bituminous coal in which Pittsburgh has the advantage in cost as respects motive power,*"* carried from our immediate shores even to the Delta of the Mississippi. Also, let not our friends, on the dangerously exposed margin of Lake Michigan, fail to recollect, that in the winter of 1814 the navigation of the Ohio river was sufficient to carry munitions of war from the Arsenal of Pittsburgh, which, arriving at a critical moment, aided General Jackson in gaining his renowned victory of the 8th of January.

It is mortifying upon this subject, to link together the high and glorious achievements of patriotism and the low and debased acts of rebellion of 1861—still, to repel the charge of deficiency, and show our facilities of intercourse, I must call up to notice how promptly Floyd fixed his traitorous eye upon the military resources of Pittsburgh, and its facility of transportation to distant and various points. And is there any man in Illinois blind to the ready distribution and conveyance of ord-

* Chicago Memorial.

nance, arms and all munitions of war, from the same workshops, to aid the patriotic exertions of the country in its present
unhappy condition?

Let me say to the people of Illinois, that I have read the
well and ingeniously written Memorial to the Government of
the United States from the citizens of Chicago, that beautiful
city, wondrous to us, but still more marvelous to the traveler
from a foreign land, who may listen to the tale of its history.
To me, the story of its origin, its growth, wealth and splen-
dor, run into the wild regions of Romance, and seem like
one taken from the Arabian Nights. Enchantment, not con-
tent with bringing up from beneath the surface of the earth
the germ of a great city, brought up one complete in all its
architecture, and crowded with a living, intelligent and en-
terprising population! Still, whilst we gaze upon, and our
minds are filled with pride by this interesting spectacle of
Western energy, we are not overcome, or frightened from the
domestic contest in which our position and homely mechanical industry induce us to engage. In our emulation (certainly
not unexpected to Illinois, as obviously appears by its select
and pointed reference to Pittsburgh), we yield all the adroit
political display spread over the sweeping geographical map
annexed to the Memorial—we yield all that enchantment, re-
ality and enterprise can bestow, with the exception of one or
two essential articles. In those, you are defective in comparison with a rival, in your notion and language, " lying on the
western *slope* of the Alleghenies." All terrestrial bounties
are not thrown in a mass on one favored spot. We yield to
you your perilous situation on the margin of a deep and beautiful lake—we acknowledge the rich soil of your extensive
plains, your beautiful prairies, resembling an unruffled ocean
of verdure and flowers—your abundant agricultural products—
the wealth of your grazing farms—the exportation of beef and
pork—your trade in lumber—your commerce in grain. You
are welcome to be called the Danzic of the Union, only do not
take from us our cherished and well-earned name. Claim—
wandering from the real point in issue—whatever you can
conveniently enumerate, and take the schedule, but leave us
the few indispensable articles for the establishment of an Ar-

mory which no impartial judgment can deny us, and which the address of the Committee can in no way include in their schedule. Bring down the whole affair to the simple and contracted point I have named—to be sure, it is one of life and death—for it is with *fire* and *metal*.

In the wide-spread schedule of which I have spoken, the Chicago Committee make one important *admission* and one important *omission*. This omission I am very far from ascribing to a want of candor. There must be a lawyer on the Committee, I discover his finger in the work. He went upon the well-known prudent professional rule, which I often practiced in my better days—when you can't answer the argument of your adversary, pass it over in silence.

The "admission" to which I make allusion is, that the coal of Pittsburgh (page 17), for steam and motive power, is superior to that of the vast extensive coal fields of Illinois, and in its cost it is less; whilst in page 17 a paragraph is inserted to assure us of the approved richness of the Illinois coal, for the very same purposes. Whilst that rich and growing State is admitted to be in possession of fields of bituminous coal more extensive than that of any other State in the Union; yet, from the pages of the Memorial, it is a little difficult to reach the accuracy of their distances from Chicago. Different points of supply are named. Sixty-five and one hundred miles are referred to as distances to the supplying and abundant mines in operation; and in page 12 we are told of the "immense coal fields lying AROUND the city." Is there an error here? Follow it up with the word "Pittsburgh," and the sentence, geographically, would be correct.

On this interesting and important article of coal, upon the present subject of investigation, why does our opposing Memorial introduce a word about the supply to Chicago from "Ohio, Lehigh, Pittston, Scranton, and the river Lehigh," in Pennsylvania? Admitting the well told account of the vast amount of coal on the Illinois and *around* the beautiful city of the Lake, does it not look a little like "carrying coals to Newcastle?" Pittsburgh never dreams of looking abroad for foreign or distant supplies—never raises her eyes to look beyond her own hills and rivers.

The "sin of omission" in the schedule to which I have referred, must have been an inadvertance. But it struck me as
a little surprising, and induced my attention, that, in the five
pages devoted "without fear of comparison," to the prominent
item of "Iron," and the variety and unlimited supply of metals to be had at Chicago, they take a sweep of seven different
States, including a portion of the territory around Lake Superior; and, to complete the variety of the collected herd, you
even include the "Scotch pigs," for the sake of what you call
the mixture. Why, then, do not the capitalists and manufacturers of Chicago arrest and turn into their furnaces the many
thousands of tons of iron and copper ore on their way from
Lake Superior to be smelted, refined and manufactured in
Pittsburgh? The Memorial observes a marked silence, certainly very significant, as to any supply or purchases from Western
Pennsylvania. Why is our city called the "Iron City" by all
around us? Why is it called by foreigners the "Birmingham
of America?" It is an oft-repeated proverb, "there is nothing in a name." But I am so partial to that old home, whose
people have been so generous to me, that I cannot avoid the
impression there is something very significant as to the workshops and materials of that home in the names it so universally bears. Let me not, by any omission, do injustice. I
confess they do mention the name of the good old common-
wealth in honorable connection with New York. They were
right to confer that honor upon us; but it was for a purpose
not at all pertinent to the present issue. It seems to have been
dragged in for the idle purpose of relating to us, that the
"Northeastern brand of grey anthracite iron" makes excellent castings for mill work!" No, no, gentlemen; leave your
distant regions, and let us return to our own homes, and ask a
question or two of our own trade and intercourse. Does not
Pittsburgh find an advantageous market at the city of Chicago
for her manufactures of iron in its most material articles—rolled,
bar, rod and sheet iron, and spikes and nails? Surely you ob-
tain such supplies from us? Is the trade ever reversed by your
greater facilities? Have you bills upon us for iron supplies?

I must hasten, my good sir, toward the conclusion of this tedious, scratched and confused letter. I will do so by some re-

marks (probably again falling into repetition) upon the most extraordinary and positive assumption of a fact to be found in the entire Chicago Memorial, and that, too, upon one of the essential points in the present inquiry—one of the most serious import—which cannot be overlooked by the Government, and must be gravely and expressly investigated and decided upon.

In pages 20 and 21 of that Memorial, the very extraordinary assertions are made, " that so long as the Government exists, this city (Chicago) must be secure;" and on page 21, "for security, she must certainly take precedence over any city in the vicinity of the Ohio river!" Could our friends have intended to attach any meaning to these extravagant assertions? Transfer Chicago from her present *outer* position, any where to the Ohio river, or its vicinity, and she loses her safety!!

Come—I take up the challenge.

Of all those many localities—for the Ohio runs a great distance, even 1216 miles, to the western boundary of Illinois—I will take the black champion to be found at the "Fork" of the Ohio, clad in *mail* of *steel* net work, with *chain* and *plate* of *iron*.

This champion, clad in such domestic armor, will not cower because he sets forth from a citadel two hundred miles from that ominous and overthrown place of arms called "Harper's Ferry," where the Chicago Committee, in tender concern for us, speak of the loss " without an effort from loyal States," as if it were a suburb of Pittsburgh. Let us turn away from that ludicrously mentioned forlorn ruin, and be serious.

Pittsburgh is held to be an unsafe position by our Chicago adversaries, because it is not " further removed than it is from the boundaries of the States in rebellion, and from Harper's Ferry, where an Armory was captured"—because " the navigation of the Ohio river is not less uncertain"—and, if possible, still more strange, because "the single trunk of rail road connecting that city with the West is not *less exposed.*"

On the question of the relative security of those two cities from *foreign* attack, the quotations just made strike my mind as strange and surprising. Probably because I am old and defective in comprehension. Still, I can see that the disgraced Harper's Ferry is 240 miles from Pittsburgh, with the ranges and spurs of the Allegheny mountains intervening; whilst the rich and tempting city of Chicago is on the line of a foreign power—that line, too, the margin of an inland sea—that nation, marine in its character—wanting in national integrity—now, as it always has been, and ever will be, full of "envy, hatred and malice" to the United States.

Pittsburgh is within a powerful State of the Union, of vast population, in close contiguity to Ohio, the third State of the thirty-four. On the South she is protected by our loyal friends of Western Virginia; her three rivers give great aid and are kindred to the surrounding beautiful and natural heights, so wonderfully adapted to fortifications and all those military works designed to be permanent, or thrown up upon any sudden alarm, or advance of a hostile force. The patriotic States of Indiana and Illinois are natural supports against any hostile assailant from the Northern side of the chain of Lakes. Pittsburgh is not upon the margin of any one of those Lakes, but many miles distant, with a valuable population intervening, securely planted in the interior of hills and rivers.

Remember how, at an early period of our history, the "Point" attracted attention as a post of military power, annoyance and defense. The Indians, the French, the English, and the Americans, contended and fought for its possession!

This comparison of relative security is quite superfluous on my part, for the Chicago map itself places Pittsburgh, in the geography of the country, in a snug corner of perfect security.

In reference to this security from foreign aggression, how stands Chicago? The question is promptly answered, not by positive and naked assertion, but simply by pointing to the spot where it stands. Is it not on the frontier? Would you build an Arsenal there to contain thousands of finished small arms, powder and ball, with hundreds of various pieces of ordnance, shot and shells? It is not surrounded by hills and heights susceptible of any kind of military works of defense? The most powerful marine nation of Europe, always in a bad and warlike humor, exercising jurisdiction over an almost illimitable domain, just across the Lake and much too near for safety—always with a strong force of regular troops in the neighborhood of the Lakes, and at this moment engaged in the erection of new fortifications in Canada. The level plain

of land all around Chicago is readily approachable by a fine
deep bay and harbor. How does it evade this danger and
establish its absolute security? It has no means of defense at
home. Its protection rests, not with the brave and patriotic
men of Illinois, but upon the hope that the Federal Government will erect vast and expensive fortifications at the Straits of
Mackinac, 200 hundred miles off, so that no power of England
would ever be able at that pass to enter Lake Michigan. Pittsburgh neither asks for or requires such public expenditures.
But if, upon a disastrous day, a hostile marine force should
happen to enter the bay of Chicago, what is then to be done?
There is no local or home defense or security. The Chicago
Memorial then tells us, if they had " the *time*," they would then
resort to the expedient of collecting the "tug boats, propellers,
steamers, and other vessels, and use them as a naval force
against Great Britain." On some desperate occasion, how we
grasp at straws. The Committee of Chicago seem to think
that in the emergency of danger to which they allude, the importance of their trade and commerce would excite the sym-
pathy of New York and Philadelphia. What further might
come, I am not able to tell, but I think all this would fail to
bring up Chicago to the standard of safety to be found at
Pittsburgh.

One word more. What does history say as to the past security of the south side of the Lakes. To be sure, I refer to a
time before Chicago had ever dreamed of spreading herself
before the gaze of an admiring world. The imbecile Proctor
had a hostile footing on our side of the Lake when defeated by
General Harrison, and Brock crossed the Strait and captured
Detroit.

Notwithstanding these facts and considerations, the Chicago
Memorial, as it approaches its conclusion, and just before it
reaches the most extraordinary offer *to buy a site* for the General Government, winds up with the wild averment, that *"for
security, she must certainly take precedence over any city in the vicinity of the Ohio River!"*

We can listen to such a proclamation, as wild as any pro-
mulgated by our Major Generals, and yet preserve a hearty
friendship for the writers of it. They atone for their mistake

upon the same page by intimating we are worthy of their competition ; that "Pittsburgh is a city of well-established character for manufacturing facilities;" our "full equality as to skillful labor, and the advantage in the cost of bituminous coal."

But for all the friendship I retain for the people of Illinois, I cannot let pass without a remark the extraordinary offer just alluded to in reference to a site. In the resolution of the House of Representatives, I can perceive no intimation that "bids" would be received, or a donation accepted as an equivalent for an objectionable site. Therefore, may I not ask, without intending any rudeness, is not the offer made to the Government an evidence of weakness? Does it not lead to a scale of "bids," rising in proportion to the unfitness of the locality? It is not possible for us to entertain the thought for one moment, such a consideration would enter into the inquiries of the Congressional Committee. Were that possible, we would feel obliged to withdraw from the contest, for we rely alone upon the truth and integrity of the exposition of our claim to the site.

In my desultory remarks to you, I have only spoken of a National Armory. But if you combine the two, an Armory and a National Foundry, our claim is greatly strengthened, and becomes at once pre-eminent. Where have ordnance, light or heavy, been cast and finished with such strength and completeness as within the limits of our city? I refer you to a letter which accompanies this paper, from Captain Rodman, a very distinguished ordnance officer and successful engineer, the inventor of many improvements in guns, the well-known patentee of the Union gun. This officer now is, and has been for many years, exclusively employed by the Government in casting and manufacture of guns. I believe he has almost the entire control and supervision of this branch of our military affairs. You will see by his letter, he does not confine himself to the limits of your resolution, but ranges over the entire Union, and fixes a large and combined establishment on the Hudson River, "a short distance above New York City." But, coming to the question, and within the limits of your inquiry, this able engineer and practiced constructor of arms, distinctly gives his judgment and opinion, that, "for a National Furnace at which gun iron can be uniformly produced of the best quality, and the fuel found together with it," he gives "the preference to Pennsylvania." He then concludes his letter by saying—"As regards *inland* sites, I know of no one that possesses greater advantages than Pittsburgh."

Where, throughout the Union, or, probably, any other country, have cast metal guns undergone and passed, triumphantly, under such long and severe tests, as those manufactured at Pittsburgh and with Pittsburgh fuel and metal?

I view the letter of Captain Rodman as entitled to some further consideration. He speaks of the comparative cost of the transportation of pig iron and that of the finished gun, and also of the supply to sea-board cities from the Hudson, at much less cost than from *any* "*inland* foundry." This hypothesis demands a remark or two.

It is true—if you have the gun cast and finished at a point on the sea-board, its *conveyance* thence to any fortification, *also upon the sea-board*, would be at much less cost than from a western inland locality. But, that is far from being the only question. We cannot escape from the essential inquiry, What was the amount of all the preliminary expenses in the "*construction*" of the gun? We of the city of Pittsburgh assert, that, taking all the expenses of the gun into the calculation, it can be sent to the distant parts of the United States at a lower cost than from any other point having manufacturing facilities.

Please to see the accompanying paper marked *B*. Also, see the weights of guns of different calibre, in paper marked *C*.

Whatever may be said in advocacy of the claim of Pittsburgh to your attention in reference to the casting and construction of ordnance, may be as equally, fairly and candidly declared upon the manufacture of small arms.

Whilst we advocate Pittsburgh and its immediate vicinity, as affording the most advantageous site for a public Armory, and give the facts, honestly believed by us to be obvious to every inquiring and disinterested mind, upon which rests the course we pursue, we trust it may not, for a moment, be thought we do not join in asserting to the Government the claim of the West for the establishment of the contemplated work. It is imperatively demanded by the present exigency of the country, and public sentiment points generally to the West, let the particular site be selected where it may.

Writing in the country this rough and hasty letter, I happen not to have upon my table a copy of the Pittsburgh Memorial. I am therefore afraid to go on and make further remarks, lest I might repeat facts and arguments already addressed to you. However, I shall proceed.

The issue raised upon the question of *locality*, sought to be obtained by the several claimants, turns, in my mind, upon a single point—the *power* to be employed. The contest lies between *water* and *steam*, supposing all other advantages, resources and facilities to be perfectly equal. A strange and bold struggle in the year 1861, between the *steam* town of Pittsburgh on the one side, and the *water* towns of Beaver and Rock Island on the other! There may have been a fair rivalship and a doubtful struggle between these two powers at a period not many years since, but now certainly gone by. The mechanism of the world has decided the question. Philosophical principles, adapted and applied to the arts, the business and labor of men, place the discovery of the availability and economy of the power of steam almost, if not at the very head of the scale of inventions of practical utility.

Water power certainly has been used, and will continue to be employed, for such purposes as the one contemplated by the terms of your resolution; but always at localities where the means and facilities of steam are not to be obtained.

If it shall be your pleasure to turn your back upon and condemn the use of the power of steam, and stand alone in the mechanical world, then hasten to the town of Beaver, (certainly possessing one of the most valuable water-falls in all the land.) Or, travel much further west, to a country of high promise, and give the site to the water power of the rapids of the Mississippi or Missouri, in the neighborhood of the city of Rock Island.

Either power—*steam*, or *water*, let the site selected be where it may—must be closely connected with the accessories and essential facilities—fuel, metals, transportation, population of artisans, &c. And if even your judgment, upon the hypothe-

ses I have mentioned, should lean in favor of the use of the
power of water, the possession of those facilities to the greater
extent would turn the scale. For instance : our well beloved
neighbors of Beaver, thinking the point I suggest a very critical and dangerous one, aim to escape from it by the very adroit
hint to be found in the last paragraph of their Memorial, but
more distinctly and at large in the extracts so indiscreetly
attached to it, taken from the report to the War Department
made by the commission in 1825. Decided as that commission
were in favor of the motive power, yet they place its success
and availability exclusively upon the command of the artisans,
facilities and resources of the city of Pittsburgh. Thus do the
military men of that commission in 1825, upon the inquiry
similar to the one before us at present, distinctly recognize the
metallic manufactures and resources of Pittsburgh. They
say :

" Comparing it with Obiophyle, it is apparent that the advantages which
would accrue to the Armory at Beaver, from its position on the Ohio
river, from its vicinity to, and *consequent command* of, *the resources* af-
forded by the city of Pittsburgh, *more than compensate for the additional cost of its water power.* * * * * To make the power, as it
ought to be, subservient to the most advantageous arrangement of the
work, will *require* the *use* of at least four steam engines, or water wheels,
in all cases. * * * And in all material respects, the position of Beaver is considered as commanding the resources of Pittsburgh."

Narrow down the limits of the question. Let the facilities
of *transportation* to and from all the points of rivalry, be considered as equal. Throw away, on the inquiry of *healthfulness*,
all our bills of mortality. Take no concern as to stone,
lime, earths, *bricks*, timber of every kind, and all materials for
buildings and shops. These materials are abundant everywhere. The industry of our country spreads skill and artisans
in every direction. What remains? *Fuel* and *Metals*. Where
are they to be found ? They are as indispensable to an Armory as air and water to the life of man. Where are they to
be found at hand—the more abundant and the more cheap?
The answer decides the question of the power to be employed
in the working of those materials.

That the character of our town directly answers the question can be no objection to the truth of the position. We advocate the adoption of that power which has changed the face of nearly the whole of the civilized world. It has usurped the power of the winds of heaven. It defies the perils of the tempest, and takes the place and performs the duties of the sails of the adventurous ship upon all the broad waters of the world. It gives irresistible force and velocity, and decisive efficiency, to our own and European ships of war; and upon fortifications and other positions upon land, in attack and defense, it is used and advancing as the great engine of war.

Come down from these high objects and purposes to which the power of steam is applied, and let us look at it in its *quiet* employment, as it were, when used for domestic and mechanical purposes.

Its *efficiency*, the Falls of Beaver will admit, and even the Rapids of the mighty Upper Mississippi will not deny.

Its *availability* for any purpose, and in any position, is proved by universal acknowledgment and adoption.

Its *docility*—its easy management, places it under the control of almost any one. Its *enginery* is now so universally known and practiced, that its machinery is almost as familiar to us as household words.

This power can be *carried* and *placed anywhere.* Choose your *site*, and *there* you have the power, let it be on high or low land, on the bank of a river, on a hill, in town, or out of town, at the mouth of a coal pit, or on an iron ore bank. But, at this day of iron machinery, choose a water-fall and you are at the mercy of that cascade! There the Government must go, let the site be suitable or not—the ground and circumstances around fit, or repulsive. "Mahomet must go to the mountain."

The *uniformity* of this power of steam? Drought and flood have no influence upon it. Winter and summer—heat and frost—are all equally harmless. Whilst it drives machinery it spreads *heat* amongst the workmen in every direction and to any extent.

This popular power may be, by a touch of the workman, or engineer, increased or diminished, at will, as business or economy may require.

When speaking of the easy and convenient mobility of the

steam engine, I might, with propriety, and fairly in connection with our subject, have said that it could very readily be placed in a situation quite contiguous to the present "Allegheny Arsenal," and at a cost by no means extravagant. Such contiguity of kindred works would give reciprocal aid and facilities to each other, and be productive of economy and success to the proposed manufacture of national arms.

Convenience as to the easy *distribution* of *power* is altogether with *steam*. It may readily be distributed over a large space by multiplying the engines, which can be located at pleasure, whilst the fixed location of the *water* compels its power to be confined.

Adopt *water* as your motive power, and yet in the midst of your numerous hands and various and complicated machinery, you cannot dispense with heat and steam—their use and application.

The liability to stoppage and suspension is greater in the use of a water-fall, than in that of a steam engine.

The repairs are the more quickly and easily made where the steam power is used, particularly where it is located in a busy community of skillful steam workmen and steam engineers, always surrounded by the implements and the various parts of the engine. A very short time is adequate to the restoration of an obstructed steam engine.

Whilst it may require chosen and selected fuel for the manufacture of iron and of ordnance, and for metal castings, almost any rough and refused fuel may be used for creating heat and steam.

Beaver certainly does, and so, I presume, does Rock Island city, depend upon Pittsburgh, very essentially, for the metal and machinery to put in operation their water power The transportation in either case would likely cost more than the simple steam engine at Pittsburgh.

When you get on, and come to the very point of starting the water power, the account certainly stands against it; that balance is, too, increased by charging the indispensable item of heating extensive workshops and buildings; and when you have the water you can't get along without steam engines. (See the report of 1825 as to the steam engines necessary to make the

Beaver Falls subservient to the purposes of a National Armory.)

Well, at this starting point, whilst you lose in other particulars, you simply save the expense in the fuel used for creating heat, and that, also, where it is required for other objects; not a very alarming expense when fuel is at hand, cheap and abundant!

Where do you find the steam engine discarded, and the water power substituted? No where. But instances of the reverse everywhere.

This letter feebly attempts to draw your attention to a subject interesting to districts, localities and cities of the ambitious West. You and others may find, I cannot, language to express the emotions excited when the eye of an American extends its gaze over the robust growth, population and rich resources of those cities. The glorious spectacle is too much for me!

I well recollect, when a boy, I stood on the eastern bank of the Allegheny, where now rests the abutment of the beautiful wire suspension bridge (no doubt taking my full share of the fright), and witnessed the Delawares and Shawnees, in full war dress (and yet with but a single scanty garment), plundering the cabin of an early and adventurous pioneer. All beyond was then a wilderness—a wild, luxuriant forest—holding out overpowering temptations to the axe and the plow of the "pale face men." Yes, those allurements civilization could not resist: and how soon were the foot-prints of the moccasin in the narrow and winding trail of the "wild red hunter" trampled out by the track of the impatient emigrant, the plowman, the artisan, and the builder of cities!

And now, in amicable temper, and united in loyalty, those very cities, in emulation and the pride of their growth, rise up in eager contest, like youthful heirs impatiently yearning to enjoy an anticipated inheritance, and grasp at the possessions and estate of a muscular parent, Pennsylvania. She very naturally resists, and claims protection from the neutral and overruling policy of that one common Government, for which her steadfast love has never fluctuated; and at this moment of national calamity, she points to that noble sentiment, which flowing like a wave of patriotism, sweeps over her entire domain, and buries deep in the ocean of oblivion the very last drift of political partisanship!

I have the honor to be, Sir, with high respect, your ob't. and humble servant,

WM. WILKINS.

Hon. J. K. Moorhead, House of Reps.

In corroboration of some general assertions relative to metals, &c., made by the Hon. Judge Wilkins, in the foregoing letter, the following Reports of several Sub-Committees, appointed from the General Committee, are presented:

Report of the Sub-Committee on Iron.

Hon. William Wilkins:

Sir—Your Committee beg leave respectfully to report, that they have given the subject committed to them, their careful consideration, and to submit the following statement of what seems to them the proper line of argument on the question. It will be observed that we have endeavored to keep as closely as possible to the subject to which our attention was called; but the question of Fuel was so intricately mingled with the Iron question, that we were forced to take at least a partial view of it, that is to say, in its bearing on the cost and quality of the iron produced here and elsewhere. We have, also, been obliged to refer to the question of freight or cost of transportation, but both these questions—of fuel and transportation—are so important as to demand separate and special attention.

In considering the materials needed by the Government for a National Armory and Foundry, it must be remembered that the two require entirely different articles of supply, and radically different classes of operators. An Armory, by which term is meant a manufactory of small arms, such as muskets, rifles, sabres, swords, bayonets, pistols, &c., needs *wrought* iron and steel, and for gun and pistol stocks, such woods as walnut, maple, and mahogany, and also proper fuel for smiths' forges and motive power. A Foundry, on the contrary, needs only *pig* or *cast iron*, or bronze, and proper fuel to melt it. If there should be added to it a manufactory of gun carriages for field or fortification, then it needs hickory, white oak, locust, &c., or what is called wagon stuff, and wrought iron for mountings. A Foundry also needs a turning and boring shop, to finish the rough guns. We shall consider the requisites for the Armory and Foundry, therefore, separately.

Let us first consider our capabilities for the supplies for an Armory. In the great requisite of Wrought Iron, we claim that it can be produced here of any required quality and quantity, cheaper than in any other locality in the Union. We have here to choose from, for the manufacture of wrought iron, the product of the mines of Eastern and Western Pennsylvania, Ohio, New York (strange as it may seem, large quantities of New York iron, in ore, pig, bloom and bar, are sold in our market), Kentucky, Tennessee, Michigan and Missouri, with the best and cheapest fuel in the known world to work it. That wrought iron can be made here better and cheaper than any where else, is proved by the fact that of all the bar iron (we mean merchant bar,) rolled in the United States, amounting, according to Leslie's Guide, up to 1856, to 240,000 tons, Pittsburgh alone produces over one-fourth of the whole. Says Leslie, on page 798 :

"The entire product, in 1856, of the rolling mills of the United States, was 498,081 tons, of which Pennsylvania made 241,484 tons. Of the 498,081 tons, 141,555 were rail road bars, leaving 356,526 tons as the product of merchant bar, &c.; but of this, it is estimated that 116,526 tons are consumed in the manufacture of nails, boiler plates, sheet, &c., leaving 240,000 tons as the bar or merchant product of the United States."

If Mr. Leslie's figures are correct, and we think they approximate very closely to the truth, Pittsburgh produces nearly *one-third* of the entire production of the United States, other than rail road iron, as will be seen from the following statistics, *obtained by actual canvass* in 1856, and published in 1857 in " *Pittsburgh as it Is.*" Says that authority, speaking of the twenty-five iron and steel works in Pittsburgh :

"These mills consume

105,333	tons of	Pig Iron.
27,267	"	Blooms.
4,931	"	Scrap Iron.
2,550	"	Swedes and Rolled Iron.

They produce as follows:

    3,212½ tons of Boiler Iron.
    67,100   "   Bar of various sizes.
    5,637   "   Sheet Iron.
    699,762   "   Nails, Spikes and Rivets.
    10,000 boxes Tacks.
    800 tons Galvanized and Imitation Russia Iron.
    10,850   " Blister, Plow, Spring and Cast Steel."

As to Lumber, all the native woods, walnut, maple, &c., can be had here as cheap, if not cheaper, than any where else, as the forests of the neighborhood and of the valleys of the Allegheny and Monongahela abound in these woods. The foreign woods, mahogany, &c., can, of course, be had here cheaper than at any other western point, as we are nearer the sea-board and have less freight to pay. But the great and predominant advantage we have, is in the fuel, not only for raising the steam for the motive power, but also in the fuel for the more important need, the smiths' forges. We have here the only coal in the United States of A No. 1 quality, for this purpose. East of the mountains, they use imported Liverpool or Pictou coal, or the coal of our vein; but west of Pittsburgh, the use of Pittsburgh coal is almost universal. From the copper and iron mines of Lake Superior to the sugar plantations of Louisiana, every little smiths' fire is dependent on the coal of the great vein of which this is the centre. It is true, that they have in Illinois an immense coal field, said to be the largest in the world; but utterly unfit for iron purposes, or why do the people living directly on this coal field, send to Pennsylvania for the coal and coke for their foundries and smith fires?

So much, then, for the Armory. Suffice it to say, if an Armory or manufactory of small arms, in addition to the one at Springfield, Massachusetts, is decided to be necessary, then our claim is, that we have here all the requisites more perfectly combined than any other location.

Let us, in the second place, consider our capabilities for the supply of a National Foundry. The guns to be made in this are all *cast*, and are what are commonly called CANNON. They are all made either of iron or bronze, the latter, however, being but a very small proportion of the guns made.

We are well aware that cast steel guns are also made, but these, of course, can be best made by contract with private individuals ; and we do not presume that the intention of the Government is, for the present, at least, to include this branch in the National Foundry. We would say here, also, that if such guns are desired, the ingots, or cast steel block from which they are forged and finished, can be produced here in any required quantity, and that heretofore they have not been produced satisfactorily any where else in the United States, while one firm, at least, in this city, has filled an order for them satisfactorily.

For the manufacture of the ordinary guns or cannon, the requisite materials are cast or pig iron of the proper quality, and the peculiar fuel to melt it. A very serious error, in all the calculations which we have seen on this subject, is in leaving out of the question the *peculiar* qualities of the iron and the fuel necessary for this purpose. Thus, in the Chicago Memorial, they lay great stress on the alleged fact, that their contiguity to the iron deposits of Lake Superior and to the coal fields of Illinois, will enable them to furnish pig iron at a lower figure than it can be produced elsewhere. This allegation could be proved erroneous in several vital points, if it were worth while to waste the time, but it is useless to "break butterflies on the wheel." Let us, for the sake of the argument, admit their allegation, however false it may be, and what does it amount to ? Nothing ! Lake Superior iron has nothing to do with this question, for the simple reason, that it has been proved conclusively, by careful and thorough experiment, that Lake Superior iron will not answer at all for heavy ordnance. By reference to the United States Ordnance Manual, last edition, page 24, it will be seen what are the requisites for pig or cast iron for guns. They are elasticity, tenacity, extensibility and incompressibility or hardness. And for this purpose, experience has shown that they are required in the following formula of proportions, or as near to it as possible :

Elasticity, involving the least set,.............................	50 per cent.
Extensibility, or capacity to resist repetition of strain,.	30 "
Tenacity, or tensile strength,.........	12 "
Hardness, or incompressibility,.	8 "

100

The object, then, in getting a pig iron from which to cast ordnance, or large and heavy cannon, is to find one that comes nearest to the above formula. All irons made from magnetic ores, of which are all the ores of Lake Superior and Missouri, are so deficient in the first and most important element, elasticity, as to render them entirely unfit for gun purposes. They are admirable for wrought iron, and have in the pig great tensile strength, but as will be seen above, tensile strength is a very insignificant item in the formula. But there is another and a fatal objection to these irons, however manufactured in the smelting process, and that is a peculiarity of shrinkage when cast, which prevents a homogeneousness of the mass. By reference to the Ordnance Manual before quoted, it will be seen that this is *the* great requisite; not only that each gun shall be homogeneous in itself, from breech to muzzle, but that all the guns in an army or a fortification shall be of equal endurance and capacity, according to their calibre. The cast iron made from magnetic ores has been found, after years of experiment, so deficient in this, the great requisite, as to force the Ordnance Departments, not only of our own, but of foreign nations, to decide, as is expressly said in the Manual referred to, that the irons made from magnetic ores are unfit for ordnance purposes. So much for the irons of Lake Superior and Missouri. They are good for certain purposes, but not for this; although admirable for wrought iron, they lack fatally the great requisites for this particular use. The unscientific idea, that it is merely tensile strength that is required in iron for all purposes, is, or ought to be, by this time exploded. Iron is never pure; all our irons, of whatever character, are alloys. In these alloys the different earths, metals, &c., &c., change the characteristics of the iron combined with them, and render one alloy fit for one use and another for an entirely different use; but for this particular use, it has been found by experience that the iron or alloy which approaches in its characteristics nearest to the above formula, is the best.

It has been found, also, by long and careful experiment, that the irons made with charcoal from the brown hematile ores of the eastern slope of the Allegheny Mountains, in the counties of Blair, Bedford, Huntingdon and Centre, of the State of

Pennsylvania, combine these requisites in a much near proportion to the formula than any other known irons; and the correctness of the formula is proved by the fact that the guns made of these irons have shown, in actual service, a capacity and endurance beyond any others. The ores to produce these irons, have not been discovered except in this one locality, which, however, is so extended, being some 600 square miles at least in extent, as to afford an abundant and inexhaustible supply. The pig iron for ordnance must, according to the Government regulations, be smelted with *charcoal* and *cold blast;* but after this smelting process, it is necessary to melt it again in order to cast it into the required shapes. For this, another and different fuel is required, and this can be found nowhere in the same perfection as at Pittsburgh. It requires twelve bushels of Pittsburgh coal to melt a ton of iron in an air furnace (not a cupola). Iron melted in a cupola is unsafe for guns. We claim, then, that the heavy ordnance, no matter where the location of the Foundry may be, must be made of Pennsylvania pig iron, and worked with Pittsburgh coal. When it can be shown that all the materials can be taken from or through Pittsburgh, and carried to any western point, and the guns reshipped through Pittsburgh to the sea-board, where the majority of them will be needed for sea-coast defense and naval use, then, of course, the Foundry should be placed at the point showing these "desiderata;" but we think we can safely wait for this until the perpetual motion is in successful operation.

If bronze guns are desired, at no point in the country is copper so abundant and so cheap, as will be seen by the accompanying report on copper. The tin being imported, can, of course, be had here cheaper than at any point west of Pittsburgh.

All of which is respectfully submitted.

> J. H. SHOENBERGER,
> ISAAC JONES,
> J. C. BLAIR,

December 26th, 1861.   *Committee.*

4

Report of the Sub-Committee on Copper and Steel.

Steel.

Hon. Wm. Wilkins, *Chairman;*

Sir—The manufacture of Steel in all its varieties, from the lowest description to the very finest material needed for tools requiring the keenest edge, and the highest temper and finish, is one of the leading pursuits of Pittsburgh.

The present annual capacity of the steel works of this city is ascertained to be about 5,350 tons of best cast steel, and 14,850 tons of all other kinds. Several of the establishments where this is made, confine their operations principally to the best sheet and bar cast steel, hammered and rolled, in direct competition with the imported or Sheffield article; and it is now very generally conceded, that the best cast steel made in Pittsburgh, is superior to the best English, in all the essentials of quality, strength, uniformity, and capacity to temper well. At the same price, it is preferred before all foreign brands, by large numbers of manufacturers of the Eastern States, as well as west of the mountains. Indeed, the reputation of Pittsburgh steel is now beyond the reach of the furious attacks of the agents for the sale of Sheffield steel, so lavishly bestowed about the time the Morrill Tariff became a law.

The Pittsburgh Committee of Steel Refiners met their antagonists at that time, before the Senate Committee on the Tariff. Samples were then exhibited, and the foreign agents were challenged to a trial of quality, which was not accepted by them, for the reason, that they were fully aware that nothing would be gained for their side in such a contest. So confident were the representatives of the steel refiners of Pittsburgh, of their ability to compete successfully in price and quality with Sheffield made steel, that they only asked of Congress to levy a mere revenue duty on their commodity, although equally entitled to protection with other important branches of American manufactures.

The most abundant testimonials are at hand, from manufacturers of steel goods all over the country, to prove what is here alleged in favor of the excellence of Pittsburgh steel. Amongst these will be found the recommendations of manufacturers of arms throughout New England and the States of Pennsylvania, New Jersey and New York, for milling tools, dies, drills, revolvers, muskets, rifles, carbines, gun locks, sword blades, bayonets, &c., also, of forks, hoes, cutlery, saws, files, reapers, edge-tools, nail cutters, skates, drills for miners' use, &c.

A notable instance of the superiority of Pittsburgh steel is thus related: The most extensive manufacturer of edge-tools in New England sent an agent abroad to procure a better quality of steel than that usually exported to this country. One large establishment in Sheffield, by the exclusive use of the best quality of Swedes iron, produced an article of the required quality. On his return to this country, the agent visited Pittsburgh, and compared this superior quality of English cast steel with that made here, from our own iron, and the consequence is, that the house he represents was so well satisfied, that large shipments of Pittsburgh steel are now made weekly to this concern, to the exclusion of the English article.

No description of steel is excluded from the variety made in Pittsburgh, and large orders are being constantly filled here for decarbonized steel, a peculiar quality used in the manufacture of rifle and pistol barrels.

Steel cannon, which in all probability will soon come into extensive use in this country, by reason of the supposed superiority of this material over brass for endurance and economy, are also made here, and several field batteries are now being constructed for the use of Government. In this department, whether it may be determined to finish the guns in the public workshops, or by private contract, the ingots, of proper weight and size, ready for hammering, turning and boring, can be supplied in any reasonable quantity, with the present facilities; and these are ready to be augmented, subject to no limit except that of the wants of the Government.

Pittsburgh is now by far the largest producing point, in the manufacture of cast steel, in the United States, and is the only place where its production has ever been attempted, west of the mountains.

The rapid increase of this particular branch of business in this city during the last two years, has been such, as to make it perfectly apparent, that we are no longer dependent upon England and Germany for this highly important element in the manufacture of implements of war. Neither can it be doubted that our productive capacity is adequate to the present demand, which is still largely influenced by foreign competition; but if a contingency should arise whereby this country should be compelled to depend upon its own unaided resources for a sufficiency of this essential material, Pittsburgh alone has the means and skill to enlarge the product in steel of every description, to the necessary standard, to supply both the Government and people with every pound that may be needed, before the stock on hand shall be exhausted.

The prices correspond with similar reputed qualities of imported steel, and range from $4\frac{1}{2}$ cts. per lb. to 15 cts. per lb., for the best cast steel, with a proportionate increase for extra small or large size bars, suitable for drills, dies, &c. It follows then, as a necessary consequence, that if any other Western point shall be selected as the proper site for a National Armory, such locality must inevitably be tributary to Pittsburgh for the all essential and indispensable material of steel, in the manufacture of machinery, arms, and other implements of war.

Copper.

This metal is also pre-eminently a Pittsburgh staple. Several of the most flourishing and successful Lake Superior mines are managed and chiefly owned in Pittsburgh. It was here, in conjunction with certain parties in Boston, that the great copper mining enterprise of Lake Superior was first projected. Its results have been such as to astonish the whole civilized world, by the discovery of masses of pure native copper, of hundreds of tons weight, in a single mass in numerous instances, whilst others of ten up to fifty tons, are matters of almost daily occurrence. From this source the material wealth of the country has been increased by many millions of dollars, and large profits annually distributed amongst the stockholders in the mines.

There are two extensive copper smelting works here, besides another at Cleveland, chiefly owned in this city, in which the product of the Pittsburgh mines is treated and refined. The amount of copper shipped from these mines alone, during the past year, is about 2,508 tons, the yield of which, when smelted, will be about 1,750 tons of refined or ingot copper; or about one-fifth of the entire consumption of the United States.

About one-half of this quantity is rolled and manufactured into the various forms for braziers' use, in two large rolling mills, exclusively employed in the business, and the remainder is sent to New York and sold for home consumption or export, principally to France, where it is held in high estimation as the best copper in the known world. The copper of Lake Superior is found to be remarkably free from foreign deleterious matter, is more ductile, and its tensile power greater than that of Cuba or South America. It is also susceptible of a much higher polish, and the brass made from it is altogether superior to any other copper in use.

A distinguished officer of our army, engaged in the manufacture of heavy ordnance for Government, has, after many severe tests, pronounced the produce of the Cliff Mine, which is refined and rolled in Pittsburgh, the best copper in the world for cannon.

Pittsburgh, therefore, stands unrivaled for the cheapest and best material for brass cannon and military equipments, and, indeed, for every other purpose to which copper can be fairly applied.

These statements do not rest upon mere assertion, but are attested by the testimony of the officers of the mines managed in this city, from whom the facts are derived. The copper of these mines is sold in Pittsburgh at from three-fourths of a cent to one cent per pound less than is obtained for the same article in New York, in consequence of the saving in the cost of transportation and other charges, and the very moderate expense incurred in the important item of fuel in refining and manufacturing.

All of which is respectfully submitted.

JAMES M. COOPER,
THOMAS M. HOWE,
F. R. BRUNOT,
ISAAC JONES,

December 26, 1861. *Committee.*

Report of the Sub-Committee on Motive Power.

HON. WILLIAM WILKINS:

SIR—In regard to Motive Power required either for an Armory or a Foundry, a great deal has been said, and your Committee think, a great deal too much, and that an undue importance has been given to this branch of the subject. It would hardly seem necessary at this day, to argue the relative cheapness of water and steam power, as the experience of the world has decided that steam, except in a very few isolated localities, has all the advantage. We shall not, then, go into the general question of the comparative merits of the two powers, but confine ourselves to the particular question before us, and give the figures.

As far back as 1825, a Commission of United States Engineers, making a report on the location of a National Armory, say there was, at that date, "at Pittsburgh, fourteen engines of from twenty to eighty horse power, whose powers exceed that of the whole extent of the Muskingum, with a head of eight feet."

The same United States commission estimate that the running of four engines—the number stated as necessary for an Armory—would cost for 313 working days, $3,255.60; in which amount they put down the cost of 160 bushels of coal fuel in 1825, at $4.80 per day, or $1,502.40 per annum—whereas, at the present day, it would cost but $2.85 per day, or $892.05 per annum—reducing the total cost to $2,363.55.

To show how small an actual horse power of the gigantic force of steam is required in the operations of an Armory, and how idle is any serious consideration of water power in the matter, we cite as a fact illustrative, that at one of the machine shops at Pittsburgh, now engaged, in common with others, in turning, boring and rifling cannon—from twelve to fifty pounders—the motive power is an engine of twelve horse power only—so rated when 100 pounds of steam are carried. The actual head of steam used in the daily running, is only twenty-five pounds, reducing the real steam force employed in driving the machinery of the establishment, to three horse power.

An engine of that small force, with 100 pounds of steam, being sufficient not only to drive the apparatus daily used for turning, boring and rifling the twelve to fifty pounder guns, but to propel, at the same time, all the various shafting, &c., necessary for the other labors of this establishment—among which is a planer of sufficient capacity to rifle the largest cannon made, as well as the lathes and machines necessary for the employment of seventy-five men.

The data cited from the United States commission of 1825, giving four engines of one hundred horse power each as sufficient for the working of a National Armory, is founded on the force of engines as constructed thirty-nine years ago, and the power required to drive machinery of the style of that date. Since then, the improvements in the steam engine have made those of from forty to fifty horse power of more efficiency in the driving of machinery, than those of one hundred horse power, constructed forty years ago. An equal gain has been made in efficiency of machinery, by improvements therein, in the same lapse of time, rendering it indisputable, that if four engines of one hundred horse power, were deemed necessary forty years ago, one of the same rating, or four of twenty-five horse each, would be more than sufficient now.

But let us leave calculation and come to actual fact. A responsible firm in this city offers to build and put in position, an engine, with boilers, pipes, pumps, stacks, &c., all complete, capable of driving one hundred lathes, for $2,500, first cost; and will also guarantee, that at present prices of coal, the fuel to run it shall not cost over one dollar per day of ten hours. Four engines of this capacity would furnish all the power (and a surplus,) for the production of 200,000 rifles or muskets per annum. The first cost of them would be only $10,000, and the cost for fuel four dollars per day, or for 250 working days, $1,000 a year. The interest on the cost of dams, races, forebays, water wheels, gates, &c., per annum, would amount almost to the first cost of the engines, and the expenses of keeping them up would far exceed the cost of the fuel for the engines. Another great advantage which steam has over water is this: the power required must be distributed over a vast amount of surface, and a great variety of speeds and of powers in order to reach all the lathes, &c., are requisite. If water is used, this involves an enormous expense in the shape of conductors of water to the different wheels, races to carry off the surplus water, water wheels, &c.; or if one large water wheel is used and all the power taken from it, then the shafting, gear wheels, pulleys, belts, &c., necessary for the proper distribution and regulation of this power, will cost several times as much as the first cost of the engines, and the expenses of keeping up this machinery, many times more than the cost of the fuel for the engines. The steam engine, on the contrary, can be so adjusted as to meet the requirements of each particular branch, in locality, power and speed. Another advantage is, that if it is the desire to suspend operations in any one or more departments, it can be done with a corresponding decrease of cost of power, with steam; while with water, the entire expense of maintenance goes on, whether the power is used or not.

Water power is not reliable; it is subject to numerous accidents, high and low water, freezing in winter, leaks in dams, races, &c.; but the steam power is always reliable—an accident to the machinery, with proper use, ought not to occur, and if so, only disables a small part of the establishment, and is readily repaired; while an accident to the water power, stops the whole until repaired.

In conclusion, your Committee would call attention to the following facts in relation to the only Armory which now belongs to the Government, the one at Springfield, Massachusetts. This Armory was originally driven by water power, and part of it is still, for a few months in the year, so driven. It is certain, that the inducement for locating the Armory there, was this water power. What is the present motive power used in this (favored by Government) locality? The largest portion of the work is done in shops using steam, and at the old shops they find the water power so unreliable, that steam engines are now being substituted in its stead. This is, it must be remembered, where steam costs (in fuel,) six times as much as at Pittsburgh.

All of which is respectfully submitted.

JOHN C. BLAIR,
GEO. H. THURSTON,
Committee.

December 26th, 1861.

At a meeting of the citizens of Pittsburgh, held at the Rooms of the Board of Trade, December 17, 1861, a Committee was charged with the duty of having the claims of Pittsburgh properly presented to the Congressional Committee who are considering the subject of a National Armory west of the Allegheny Mountains. The foregoing papers relating thereto having been read before the Committee, were ordered to be printed in pamphlet form, as auxiliary to the duty assigned them. In addition to the general facts mentioned in these papers, the Committee add:

That all sites asking to be chosen as the location of a National Armory and Foundry, present, as arguments in favor of their selection, certain presumed advantages of site, minerals, labor, transportation facilities, geographical position, &c. These advantages exist, possibly, at all the rival locations, to some extent, either singly or in combinations; but they are only valuable so far as they are superior to similar ones existing at other points, or as forming at any one location, the largest combination of those advantages the most to be desired for the site of a National Armory and Foundry. The existence of any one special advantage, with the exception of fuel, however great its magnitude, at any certain location, would not justify its selection, to the necessity of transporting to it all other requisites; nor would reason support the rejection of a site where all desirable qualities largely existed, in favor of one where two or three advantages only combined to a limited degree.

That in some of the cities and towns striving to secure in their midst the location of the Governmental Workshops in question, there do exist certain isolated and limited advantages, is not to be denied; nor is it any the less to be denied that the claims of others are but reflections of advantages existing elsewhere; from whose shadow it is sought to create, by ingenious argument or bold assertion, the substance of things desired. To hunt up these scattered qualifications, in order to contrast

5

them with the compact and vast combinations of all desired requisites self-evidently existing at Pittsburgh, were a waste of time and labor.

The full examination of the advantages asserted by Chicago, contained in the preceding pages, renders it unnecessary that those of any other Western claimant should be, in a similar manner, or to any extent, analyzed. The weakness of Chicago in all the points of fuel, metals, and general manufacturing facilities, is a weakness shared by all Western localities. The strength of Pittsburgh, as contrasted with Chicago, is even greater in comparison with other Western rivals; and it would be but a long reiteration of facts, figures and statements, to present, in a fair side by side contrast, the complete and real advantages of Pittsburgh, with the isolated and shadowy ones of other Western claimants of the National Armory and Foundry.

Upon the possession of water power, great stress is laid by the citizens of some of the locations designated as desirable sites. In a day and generation past and gone, water power would have been an advantage worthy of argument. In an era of manufacturing, unblessed by the economic power of steam, it would have been precious; but that in the present day of scientific industry it should have been seriously set forth as a manufacturing advantage, is so absurd as to render it unnecessary that it should be discussed to any extent, as of influence in controlling the selection of a site for a National Workshop.

Those persons who cling fondly to old traditions, and consider water power—with its unreliability of force, cumbersomeness and cost of construction, recurring and prolonged seasons of repair—superior to the compact, reliable, cheap and enduring steam engine, are referred to some remarks upon the comparative cost and availability of water and steam power, in this pamphlet.

The history of metals shows that they seek the point where the fuel required for their working is cheapest, most copious, and of the best quality, and that at such a point they are most cheaply manufactured. Pittsburgh is such a point.

The wants of an Armory and Foundry demand that it should be located where the supply of metals required, shall be in the greatest abundance, of the most desirable qualities, of the easiest access, and at the cheapest prices.

The commerce of the South and West, the manufactories and private armories of the East, even the demands of European arsenals, render it indisputable that Pittsburgh is such a point ; a fact fully substantiated by the articles on Iron, Steel and Copper, printed in these pages.

The geographical location of a National Armory and Foundry should be where a condition of things opposite in the extreme exist—where it may be inaccessible—where it shall be accessible. The topography of the country shows that Pittsburgh is a natural stronghold, and can be made impregnable to an invading foe; while the facts in relation to its great transportation facilities to all sections of the country, prove its accessibility. The possible emergencies of an Armory and Foundry, demand that it shall be located where the largest supply of labor skilled in the working of all metals exists—where the greatest variety of mechanics permanently reside. It will not be denied that Pittsburgh has the greatest supply of labor skilled in working all the metals used in manufacturing munitions of war, and the greatest variety of mechanics.

The requirements of an Armory also render it desirable that it should be located where woods, suitable for arms, abound— where leather is plenty—where health is secure. The exposition of the claims of other localities, has shown how Pittsburgh abounds in these requirements.

By the examination of certain alleged manufacturing advantages presented by Chicago, and through those of that city, similar ones claimed by other points, we have endeavored to answer, by comparisons, the question, Where should a National Armory and Foundry be located in the West ?

The prior portion of the title of this pamphlet, "Does the Country require a National Armory and Foundry West of the Allegheny Mountains ?" is a question to whose affirmative answer we apprehend there will be but few dissenting voices. To the latter clause, "If it does, where should they be located ?" we feel, from the indisputability of the absolute dominion of the Iron City in all the demands and requirements of a National Armory and Foundry, and the subordinate

and dependent position of all Western communities upon it
for all such requirements, we may make bold to answer, AT
PITTSBURGH! sincerely asserting, and honestly believing, that
the best interests of the Government and the whole country
will thereby be most efficiently, cheaply, and securely sub-
served.

WM. WILKINS, *Chairman.*

WM. ROBINSON,	JAMES M. COOPER,
J. H. SHOENBERGER,	R. T. KENNEDY,
F. R. BRUNOT,	J. C. BLAIR,
JOSIAH KING,	ISAAC JONES,
JAMES PARK, JR.,	JOHN BISSELL,
C. G. HUSSEY,	CALVIN ADAMS,
THOS. M. HOWE,	GEO. H. THURSTON,

Committee.

www.ingramcontent.com/pod-product-compliance
Lightning Source LLC
Chambersburg PA
CBHW022031080426
42733CB00007B/798